Save Our Slides

PowerPoint™
Design
That Works

THIRD EDITION

William Earnest
St. Edward's University

Kendall Hunt
publishing company

Kendall Hunt
publishing company

www.kendallhunt.com
Send all inquiries to:
4050 Westmark Drive
Dubuque, IA 52004-1840

Printed in the United States of America
10 9 8 7 6 5 4 3 2

Contents

Special thanks to my colleagues
Teri Varner and Stephanie Martinez
for supporting this project
from the beginning

Why This Book?

Better slides by design

Presentation slides have become the most misused tool in the history of communication—which is why this book is **not** another operating manual for PowerPoint. There are too many of those already, and look where they've gotten us:

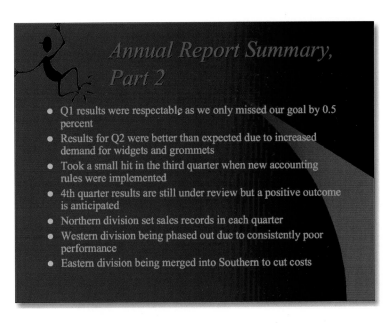

Here's a point to ponder: We're the most technologically advanced species in the history of the planet . . . and these are our slides?!

A slide like this isn't just a bad slide—it's bad communication. I repeat: This is **bad communication**. To illustrate, consider an analogy. How easy is it to extract meaning from the following sentence?

```
the jumped fox cow quickly brown over
```

Not very. A sentence written with no sense of the syntax rules that inform the language it's using—so poorly designed that it isn't even functional—is intolerable. But this begs the question:

. . . why do we put up with slides that are just as flawed?

From the standpoint of effective communication, most slides are like this one; their "visual syntax" is all screwed up. In visual media, bad communication often stems from poor design. That's where this book is different than most. It's about how to craft **better** slides by learning some useful **rules of design**.

So if the thought of having to sit and stare (or squint) at another set of hideously unhelpful PowerPoint slides is more than you can take, this book is for you. It's time to fight back.

You don't have to take it anymore.

But don't throw away your old slides. Use good design to recycle them.

A Brief Intro

Welcome to the electronic wilderness

Do you know what the differences are between slides and fire?

- Fire rarely kills brain cells
- Fire typically encourages creativity
- Fire is almost never boring
- Fire is a good thing most of the time

But to work effectively, fire has to be carefully controlled. That's why we have all kinds of rules governing its use. And that may be the single greatest difference between slides and fire:

Unlike fire, there are **no rules** for slides

Which makes the world of slideware sort of the Wild West of communication:

- No laws
- No judges
- No roads
- Lousy maps
- Too many bullets

All the West needed to tame it was a little good old-fashioned law and order—Judge Roy Bean and a few permits here and there. Basically, some rules.

Since its debut in the late '80s, PowerPoint—despite its tremendous potential for creative communication—has been a kind of electronic wilderness that we've all become lost in. What we need to set things right is a straightforward set of do's and don'ts—**a few simple rules**.

So, turn the page. It's time to lay down a law or two and bring a little civilization to this electronic frontier of ours.

I don't mean to traumatize you, but let's go back once more to that loathsome slide we looked at a couple pages ago.

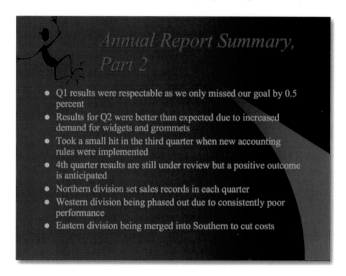

Okay, so we can all agree that we *hate* slides like this . . .

. . . but do we know why?

After all, we can't fix it if we can't clearly describe what's wrong with it in the first place. So let's start there.

From the standpoint of good design—design that helps rather than hinders the process of communication—here's the official indictment:

- a shifting shade of sleep-inducing "electric" blue
- a template older than most computers
- text that's too small to read
- a font better suited for printing than display

- cheesy clip-art (some clip-art is perfectly fine; this isn't)
- poor color contrast
- annoying animation & sound effects
- too many words in an already-crowded list of bullets

No wonder we're all sick and tired of slide-based presentations. Fortunately (and this is really, *really* important) **none of these problems is inherent in the software itself**.

Not a single one. Instead, what we're seeing is the result of misuse. In other words, it's user error—at least technically. The fact is that we're not really to blame since no one ever taught us this stuff.

Until now.

There are seven **Rules of Design** for presentation slides (i.e., those intended for big screen use in front of a roomful of people). Follow these rules and your audience is far more likely to react favorably to what you're pitching (or at least stay awake—and possibly even pay attention).

We'll start with a simple list, then drill down for more detail as we go through the remaining chapters.

Okay, the seven Rules of Design for slides are:

1 **TEMPLATES**: Choose wisely

2 **TEXT**: Know the limits

3 **FONTS**: Use sans serif typefaces

4 **IMAGES**: Make professional choices

5 **COLOR**: Pick high-contrast combinations

6 **ANIMATION**: Don't get too creative

7 **CAPITALIZATION**: Stop capitalizing *everything*

But before we get to the Rules themselves, how's about a little instant gratification to end this chapter? Let's apply these rules to transform that hideous blue slide of ours.

Look at what a few design rules can do:

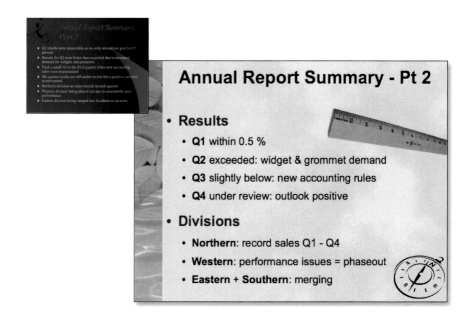

In the coming pages, each of the Rules of Design will be defined, explained, and illustrated in detail.

And because you'll continue to use PowerPoint (or its equivalent) for many years to come, I've included three **"Designer's Notebook"** entries. These pages allow you to write down the names of preferred templates, fonts, and clip-art styles. Maintain these lists and keep them handy so that as the years go by you can build on your successes and ultimately develop an enviable design style that is uniquely yours.

For better or worse, electronic slides aren't going away, so the time to start separating yourself from the rest of the pack (like those drones who think electric blue slides are "pretty") is now. Turn on the computer and get out a pen—today is the first day of the rest of your slides.

Rule 1: **TEMPLATES**

Choosing the right kind

Not all PowerPoint templates are created equal. Templates of course are those ready-made design schemes that are included with the software (they are now also known as design "themes").

When it comes to picking the right template, about 90% of the battle is knowing which ones **not** to use. But we'll start with the following general features that separate good themes from the riff-raff:

Desirable **Template Features**

- Light background color (the preferred choice)
- Uniform background color (no shifts in brightness or shade)
- Complementary, inconspicuous design elements

Not surprisingly, the telltale characteristics of bad design themes are pretty much the opposite of these. But some are worth mentioning specifically:

Bad **Template Characteristics**

- Bright or **medium** shades of blue in particular
- Medium colored backgrounds
- Backgrounds shifting from light to dark or vice versa
- Overwrought or distracting design elements
- Any template that has grown stale from overuse

The last item on that list is worth some elaboration. There are decent themes/designs that are simply overused, and for that reason alone should be avoided. Examples include Dad's Tie, Melancholy, and Cloud Skipper as well as newer themes like Civic and Concourse. If you see a theme that's used all the time, then it's time to choose another design.

Lists such as these are great, but nothing brings them to life like a good set of examples. And since the bad stuff's always more fun, that's where we'll go first. You've heard of the five people you meet in Heaven, right? Well, this is not that list. Instead, I give you the:

Six Templates from **Hell**

⊘ Soaring

Meet the oldest template in the world. There's no better way to look unoriginal and stale. Just how many shades of blue can we use at one time? And what is that—that "swoosh" thing anyway?

Seriously, *Soaring* was one of the original PowerPoint templates. It hasn't shipped with a new version of the software since Bill Clinton was in his first term as president. Yet somehow it lives on, the all-but-indestructible cockroach of templates.

So I'll give it this much—it's got staying power. But unless you want to turn your audience into a raging mob of bored zombies, don't give it the time of day.

⊘ Whirlpool

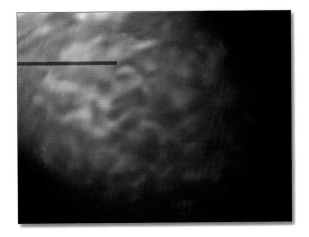

Ever wonder what the core of a nuclear reactor looks like? Or the left lobe of your brain? How about both at once? Well, now you know. Nightmarish and disturbing, your content can't compete with all that noise in the background. Ugh. So much for whirlpools being "relaxing."

⊘ High Voltage

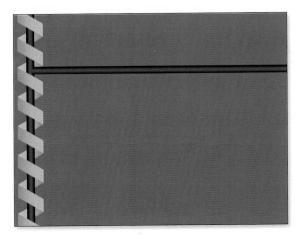

Ah, the 1950s. Mad scientists, DNA, and shades of blue so dreary that they went out of style, well, in the '50s. And don't forget about the "particle" that flies up the side tube then cuts across—on each and every new slide you open. Audiences *love* that!

⃠ Marble

Rough day at the mausoleum, dear? Not even a mortician could make this one look good. More detailed than a Seurat painting, it just may capture your audience's attention, but will always do so at the expense of your content. Always.

⃠ Fireball

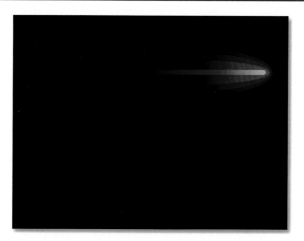

Ever had a stale potato chip? Well, think of this design as the stale potato chip of templates. The solid black background's bad enough, but the "comet's head" looks tacky by today's graphics standards. And, like *Soaring*, this one's been driven into the ground with overuse. Let it go. Time to move on.

$\oslash$ Blue Diagonal

Just what the world needs—another blue template. An old, overused one too. Not to mention the gradient shift from extremely bright to nearly black. With so many strikes against it, you'd think it would be mighty unpopular. But you'd be wrong.

Of course, there are many, **many** other design themes out there that are just as bad as (or worse than) these. But these six are worth pointing out because they teach at least two valuable lessons:

1. For reasons that defy explanation, they continue to be widely used today, numbing audiences the world over and helping to reinforce slideware's bad reputation.

2. They effectively illustrate the characteristic problems that all bad templates share. So if you come across a template that reminds you of one of these six Templates from Hell, drop what you're doing and run screaming from the room.

The news isn't all gloom and doom though. Many of PowerPoint's newer template designs seem to have gotten things just right.

Following are a few of my personal favorites. Most of these templates are versatile enough to be used in a wide variety of presentational settings, from the classroom to the boardroom.

☑ Bold Stripes

This design proves that blue can work quite well as an *accent* color on a template (using it as the whole background is the problem). The vertical pinstripes give this template a dash of subtle elegance. It may be "bold" but it's not overpowering.

☑ Network

Not much to it, is there? And that's the beauty of it. A good template is present but unobtrusive—a time-honored design principle known as *transparency*. Such templates will always let you and your content be the proper stars of the show.

☑ Profile

They don't display accurately here in print, but this template has light gray pinstripes running horizontally. Like *Bold Stripes*, this one is elegant and professional, but with a splash or two of red for a little added personality. I use this one a lot in my classroom lectures.

☑ Echo

Three dots and a line? You're probably thinking, *Well I could have designed that!* And indeed you could have. Good templates don't have to be complex or difficult to create. The only hard work is the conceptual stuff—knowing what constitutes good design in the first place.

☑ Eclipse

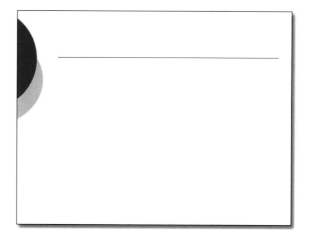

Think of this one as *Echo's* more extroverted alter ego. And if the color scheme's not your cup of tea, it's easily changed from the **Slide Master** via the **View** menu (Office for Windows).

☑ Layers

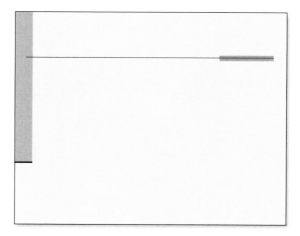

One of my all-time favorites. You'll want to change the default font for *Layers* to a sans serif typeface (the focus of Rule 3). This template's more upscale than most, making it a good choice in no-nonsense, sober, or sophisticated settings.

☑ Level

As with *Layers*, the default typestyle needs to be changed from serif to sans serif. And if earth tones aren't your thing (or it isn't harvest time yet) just change the colors of the various elements to match your specific needs.

Here's another good template, which happens to be called *Edge*. By any measure, it's pretty unassuming. If you need a low-key or straightforward quality, this is your ticket.

To illustrate how easy it is to customize any template to better suit your particular presentation's requirements, read on.

Templates like *Edge* can quickly be transformed from Plain Jane to Cinderella in just a few clicks. As noted previously, go to the menu and choose the **Slide Master** function under the **View** menu.

Once the Slide Master is open, changing things to better suit your needs couldn't be easier:

1. **Double-click on the upper gold line to change its color to whatever you want**

2. **Do the same with the lower gold line (or is it more of a mustard color?)**

3. **Insert your organization's logo or other art work, and you're all set**

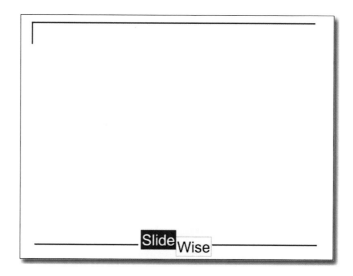

As was the case with the bad templates we looked at, there are of course many, many more good ones. But the eight mentioned here admirably illustrate the qualities that all effective template designs share. And like the changes to *Edge* shown above, all PowerPoint design themes can be easily transformed through a few simple edits to the Slide Master.

Can't find all of these templates or looking to corral a few more? A Google search should lead you to many of these old favorites, and you can check out the "Templates" section of Microsoft Office Online.

One thing you've probably noticed about these good templates is how lightly-colored the backgrounds are. That's because in most venues, **dark text on top of a light background** offers the greatest readability for the audience.

Again, that's true in most venues, but not necessarily all. Here's a list of several situations in which you might consider using a dark background template (with light-colored text):

When Dark Templates Might Work

- The room is going to be very brightly lit

- The screen has lights shining directly on it

- A light background doesn't fit the mood you need

- You want to use the organization's colors but they look ghastly against a light background

Don't get me wrong; I've seen some stunning presentations that used dark backgrounds, but in general it takes much more work to achieve results that rival what can be done with a light background. For example, it's harder to work with images and other graphics when using a dark background color (more on that in Rule 4).

If you have to use a dark background, on the following page are two templates that you might want to consider (remember to use a *light* color for the text).

These are but two of many possible choices, yet they represent their genre well. Notice that the backgrounds are composed of solid colors (no shifts in brightness) even if more than one color is used. Additional design elements are present as well (lines, etc.), but they complement rather than distract.

☑ Circuit

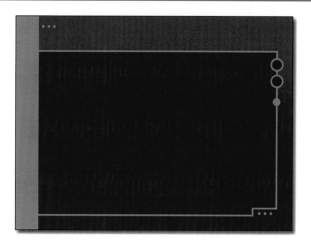

☑ Refined

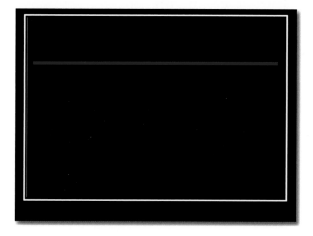

Take a moment to open PowerPoint and browse the available templates. These are now officially known as "themes" and can be found under the Design menu heading. Revisit the various choices based on the perspective you've gained from reading this chapter. As with all the Rules of Design, after you've used them for a while, making good choices will become second nature. In the meantime, to help you keep track of templates you particularly like, a Designer's Notebook entry is included on the next page.

Templates

As you come across good templates (or bad ones), keep a running list here of what works and what doesn't. Fill in or circle the stars to denote favorites. That way, five years from now when you're hammering out that career-making presentation for some big wigs at your office, you won't have to try to remember the name of that perfect template you found once upon a time but lost track of. What was it called again—*Astronaut? Astral Projection? Waldorf Astoria?*

Good Templates

	Favorite		*Favorite*
_____	☆	_____	☆
_____	☆	_____	☆
_____	☆	_____	☆
_____	☆	_____	☆
_____	☆	_____	☆
_____	☆	_____	☆
_____	☆	_____	☆
_____	☆	_____	☆
_____	☆	_____	☆
_____	☆	_____	☆

Never Use

_____   _____   _____

_____   _____   _____

_____   _____   _____

Stand and Deliver

- Position yourself as shown
- Talk to the audience, not to the screen
- Use the screen as you would a notecard—for reference only

Face the audience, at a slight angle

Turn your head, not your body, to glance at the screen

Your shoulders form a straight line to the center of the screen

Reining in wordiness

Rule 2 is one of those principles that can be summed up in a single sentence—a single sentence that every presenter should have to write on a chalkboard 500 times:

PowerPoint is not a word processor
PowerPoint is not a word processor
PowerPoint is not a word processor
PowerPoint is not a word processor
PowerPoint is not a word processor
PowerPoint is not a word processor
PowerPoint is not a word processor
PowerPoint is not a word processor
PowerPoint is not a word processor

In other words, **PowerPoint is not a word processor**. Design guru Edward Tufte describes slideware as a "low-resolution" medium, meaning that dense objects like text get lost easily. And he's exactly right. In this regard, slides are no different than a highway sign or a billboard. And when was the last time you saw a highway sign that looked like this?

Austin is the next exit. If that's your destination, you should probably get in the righthand lane and activate your turn signal.

By the time you're finished reading such a sign, you will have done one of the following:

- missed your exit
- wrecked the car
- missed your exit and wrecked the car

Of course we know that in reality the same sign would probably look more like this:

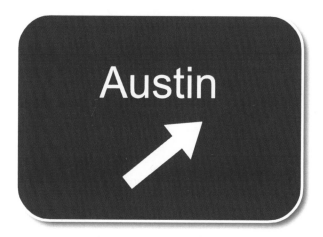

No transportation official interested in a long-term career would ever dream of misusing the road sign medium in such a ridiculous fashion—and yet we do it with slides all the time.

In fact, the #1 problem with PowerPoint is our tendency to put **too many words on slides.** If your need for text is great, use Microsoft Word instead and give your audience handouts to read. It's a much better fit, and they'll thank you for it. To sum up:

PowerPoint is a **visual** medium

MS Word is **textual**

They serve different communication functions

Here are some helpful ideas for limiting the number of words on a slide. There are actually five separate strategies that can help stem this epidemic of "verbal diarrhea," otherwise known as *verbalitis*. Don't try these on an empty stomach, and be sure to drink plenty of water.

Top 5 Ways to Cure **Verbalitis**

1. Reduce sentences to key words
2. Aim for ≤ 20 words per slide
3. Keep type sizes large enough to read
4. Use accepted symbols & abbreviations
5. No more than 6 main bullets per slide

Now let's illustrate each of these strategies in turn.

 ## 1. Reduce sentences to key words

Consider the following, all-too-typical slide. It's certainly got a bad case of verbalitis (although we've seen worse).

> ● ● ● | **Summary of Benefits Changes for the New 2006 Fiscal Year**
>
> o From now on, physicals will be required in order to increase the amount of life insurance coverage, except for new enrollees
>
> o No physical is required when requesting a decrease in life insurance coverage
>
> o Pre-existing conditions will no longer be covered for new enrollees, including dependents
>
> o List of pre-existing conditions available in benefits packet material or from HMO website

Don't bother counting for yourself, but there are **68** words on this slide. If you consider the design implications of such slides, then you've put your finger on the heart of what is most hateful about slideware. After all, here's a slide that:

- is all words
- has too many words
- has absolutely no visuals
- is supposed to be a **visual medium**

One problem at a time, obviously, and in this part of the discussion we're going to concentrate solely on reducing the number of words, specifically by using the technique of **keywording**.

There's a simple formula you can use to reduce full sentences down to their key ideas. Apply the following to the title and each bullet:

ELIMINATE:

- **articles** (*a, an, the*)
- **understood pronouns/possessives** (*we, you, your*)
- **simple verbs & infinitives**
- **repetitive phrasing**

An example will illustrate just how easy this is to do. Imagine that you're the president of Acme Grocery pitching the company's home delivery service to an audience of prospective clients. Here's your main "benefits" slide:

The Acme Grocery Pledge

- We promise to offer you only the freshest produce available

- We unconditionally guarantee your complete and total satisfaction

- We will deliver your groceries to you anywhere, anytime

Now let's apply the four steps of the keywording process and see what can be eliminated:

The Acme Grocery Pledge

- We promise to offer you only the freshest produce available
- We unconditionally guarantee your complete and total satisfaction
- We will deliver your groceries to you anywhere, anytime

Note that the phrase "anywhere, anytime" is circled because—while important as an idea and selling point—the wording is repetitive.

Now as we look at this edited version, the essence of the ideas begins to come clearly into focus. We realize we can probably eliminate another word or two (e.g., "pledge" and "promise" are synonyms) and actually spot an opportunity for **parallel phrasing** (always a good idea when various ideas are of equal importance):

Acme's Pledge

- Freshest produce

- Guaranteed satisfaction

- Unlimited delivery

In short, here's where our edits are ultimately leading us:

What started with **31** words ended up with **8**

If you're keeping score, that's a reduction in verbiage of **74%**

In the process, the main selling points became dramatically clearer—a principle so important that it's worth putting in a colored box:

> In **visual** media, **more** words does **not** equal **better** communication. Less is almost always more.

As a presenter, you should still **speak all the words** that were on the **original** version of the slide. When presenters do this, their spoken words will perfectly complement the key words their audiences see.

The principle of keywording is so central to good slide design that it's impossible to achieve success without it. You can do everything else right, but if you get this one thing wrong then the whole show is off.

In effect, keywording is the cornerstone of good design. Or at the very least, as this picture suggests, it's the **foundation** of good design.

All the other Rules of Design

Using key words

That's why text management and verbalitis in general get more ink on these pages than any other aspect of design. And without the judicious use of keywording, of course, there is no such thing as text management in the first place—only text mismanagement. So reining in word count really does hinge on this one principle.

By the way, I tried to find a picture of an actual, honest-to-goodness cornerstone to use in this discussion but it just wasn't happening. During my search I came across the stack of pebbles on the previous page and it was then that I decided to switch metaphors. I'm glad I did, but I'd still like to find a nice, garden variety picture of a cornerstone one of these days.

As a consolation prize, however, I stumbled upon this picture of the Greek Parthenon. I've studied it closely and feel sure that there's a cornerstone in here somewhere.

All rock-based metaphors aside, the keywording principle has a number of practical implications that are worth creating yet another colored box for:

- Slides are only a speaker's notes (i.e., main ideas)

- Slides are not a verbatim transcript

- No full sentences on slides except for direct quotations

- If speakers have to read from their slides, they're probably using too many words

- Slides are not a diary; speakers should be selective about what they ask the audience to look at

On that note, check out the following exercise. It'll give you a chance to put your money where your key words are.

The Joy of Keywording

Consider the following slide, which obviously has a severe case of verbalitis.

How I spent my summer vacation this past year

- I had the privilege of snorkeling in Hanauma Bay, Bimini, and Devil's Cove
- In Colorado, I rode the Durango-Silverton Narrow Gauge Railway from Durango to Silverton and back again
- I attended thirteen self-help seminars in various and sundry places in rural Canada
- From May to August, I ran three marathons and lost ninety-seven pounds

Use the strategies described on the previous pages to pare down the verbiage on this slide to its essential keywords. Do this in a two-pass process, first on the blank slide labeled Draft 1 (for obvious cuts) and then on Draft 2 (for further revisions). Don't forget to fix the slide's title in addition to the body text.

As you edit, keep three things in mind:

1. It's **okay** to change words and phrases if needed
2. It **ain't okay** to change or obscure the original meaning
3. If it helps, include visually logical elements such as:
   a. sub-bullets
   b. symbols/numbers in place of words (see p. 32)

Draft 1—Obvious cuts

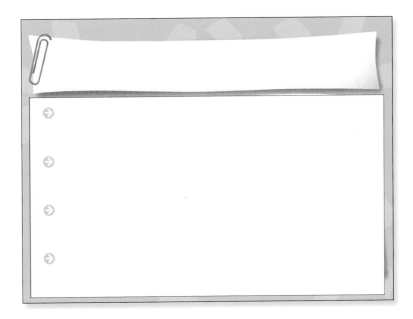

Draft 2—Additional refinements

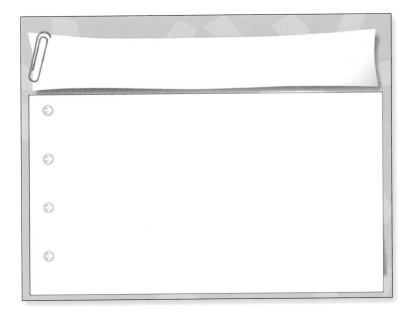

2. Aim for ≤ 20 words per slide

Now let's go back to our first verbalitis patient from a few pages back—the boring one with all those words:

 ### Summary of Benefits Changes for the New 2006 Fiscal Year

o From now on, physicals will be required in order to increase the amount of life insurance coverage, except for new enrollees

o No physical is required when requesting a decrease in life insurance coverage

o Pre-existing conditions will no longer be covered for new enrollees, including dependents

o List of pre-existing conditions available in benefits packet material or from HMO website

68 Words

Through the magic of keywording, we can now see our way clear of traps like using full sentences. Instead, we begin to consciously edit ourselves, choosing to **visually emphasize only what matters most** about each of our ideas.

● ● ● FY06 Changes

o **increase** in life coverage requires physical exam

   • exception: new enrollees

o **decrease** in life coverage – no physical required

o pre-existing conditions not covered for:

   • new enrollees (including dependents)

   • list of conditions in packet & HMO website

36 Words

The target range of ≤ 20 words per slide turns out to be a handy metric. It provides a realistic goal that works particularly well when you find yourself editing someone else's slides. In this case, going from 68 words to 36 (rather than 20) is still a dramatic improvement.

When creating your own slides from scratch, however, try to restrict yourself to the official limit of ≤ 20 words per slide. In fact, in classes my students have consistently produced their best slides—creative, memorable, and largely visual—when I require them to use **no more than 15** words on a slide.

If that sounds impossible to you, it's because you're stuck in word processor mode. Reboot and remember that slides are a—

• Visual Medium •

3. Keep type sizes large enough to read

One of the reasons we tend to put too many words on slides is that we choose type sizes that are in fact too small for use on large projection screens. And since nature abhors a vacuum, we **type**, **type**, **type** to fill up all the empty space.

Words sized at 10 or 12 points may look perfectly fine to us as we sit at our high-resolution laptop or desktop monitors, but big presentation screens operate at decidedly lower resolutions than their smaller counterparts.

Technical explanations aside, here's the bottom line when it comes to sizing text for big screen audiences:

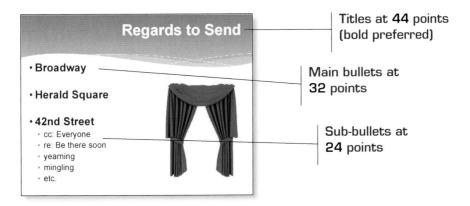

Strive for these targets. Not only do they make it easier for audiences to read what's on the screen, **they place natural limits on the number of words presenters will be able to type in the first place**.

It is virtually impossible for big screen audiences to easily process text that is rendered in sizes less than 18 points. Under no circumstances should you drop below that threshold. Consider it an absolute limit. Text displayed at less than 18 points is meant to be read on paper, not projected on screen. Remember: PowerPoint is not a word processor. (Don't make me get the chalk.)

 ## 4. Use accepted symbols & abbreviations

This one's pretty much common sense, but it's worth pointing out because I still see many instances where speakers forget to use it. The rule is simple. If there's a **commonly-accepted** symbol, acronym, or abbreviation for a word or phrase, then use it.

Remember, on-screen space is limited, so the more visual real estate you can conserve the better. Every character counts.

Instead of:	Use:
One, two, three . . .	1, 2, 3 . . .
First, second, third . . .	1st, 2nd, 3rd . . .
Quarter 1, quarter 2 . . .	Q1, Q2 . . .
Fiscal year	FY
Thousands	000s
U.S. dollars	USD
Number	# or No.
And	&
Street, Avenue . . .	St., Ave. . . .
International	Int'l.
Incorporated	Inc.
For example, et cetera . . .	e.g., etc. . . .
Television, compact disc . . .	TV, CD . . .
Texas, California, Maine . . .	TX, CA, ME . . .
Central Intelligence Agency . . .	CIA, FBI, NASA, UCLA . . .
Intelligence Quotient . . .	IQ, DNA, rpm, mph, mpg . . .
Martin Luther King, Jr. . . .	MLK, LBJ, JFK, FDR . . .

Familiar objects

Organizations known by their acronyms

Everyday acronyms

Famous peeps

And so on and so forth. I realize you don't need anyone to teach you common symbols and abbreviations. The point of including them here is simply to **remind you to do it**.

5. No more than 6 main bullets per slide

In fact, 3, 4, or 5 bullets is better, with plenty of white space in between for a little visual breathing room.

Here's the thing. It's something of an axiom in educational psychology that the average person can retain a maximum of five to seven items in short term memory. After that, things start getting lost.

Hence, it's best not to push our luck (or, more to the point, our audience's luck). Aim for **3 to 5** main bullets, and if you can't do that, make a cold stop at **6** no matter what.

A simple test will illustrate why these numbers represent a natural barrier. Mentally study the following bullet list for a minute or so (take as long as you want), until you feel comfortable that you've got it memorized.

FY12 HR Goals

- Improve employee retention strategies
- Review sabbatical policy proposal
- Expand 401(k) investment choices
- Increase ESOP limits
- Remodel daycare facility
- Hire new foodservice contractor

Ready?

Hide or flip this page under and go to the next one. **Do not look back**. That would be cheating, and if you cheat on this, well . . . probably no one will ever know (but you'll miss the point of a really enlightening exercise).

Okay, proceed to the next page!

Without referring back to the slide on the previous page, write down as many of the bullet items as you can recall:

_____

_____

_____

_____

_____

_____

_____

_____

_____

One more question:
How many bulleted lines were there in total? _____

Okay, now go back and check your answers against the original.

Odds are that you didn't get the whole list correct, a reality that has several implications. While most of these implications are not life-threatening, they're still worth knowing:

1. You're perfectly normal

2. That was "only" six things

3. Which is why the upper limit is 5 to 7 items

4. Think about how often we see slides with 11 or 12 bullets!

5. Yikes. Another symptom of verbalitis.

Note that **sub-bullets** are a different matter. We're not counting them against our total of 6 main bullets. At the same time, if a couple of main bullets have subs below them—AND you're using the proper point sizes for text—there's no way you're going to fit 6 *main* bullets into that space in the first place. This is what is known as a "self-correcting problem." Don't believe me? Check it out:

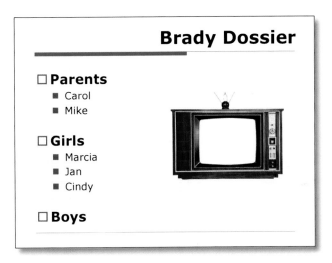

See? You can't even fit the whole Brady Bunch on a single slide. And if you thought Chez Brady was bad, try fitting the entire Walton clan on one. It just can't be done.

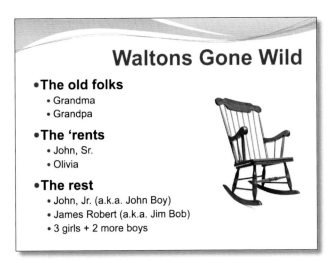

Body Talk

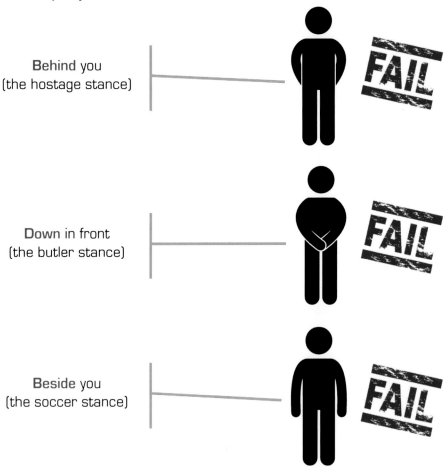

- Default hand position:
    - —Up, together, in front of your chest
    - —Place one thumb in the opposite palm
- From there, it's easy to **gesture**, **gesture**, **gesture**
- Always come back to this default position between gestures

Do NOT put your hands:

Behind you
(the hostage stance)

Down in front
(the butler stance)

Beside you
(the soccer stance)

Rule 3: **FONTS**

Think about your own handwriting for a moment. You know how you do that cute little thing with your Ys and how people are always saying your Cs look like Os?

Well, fonts are to computers what handwriting is to people—we use them to give electronic type a consistently uniform appearance. Otherwise, imagine how difficult it would be to visually process even the simplest sentences:

See Spot run.

Granted, it might make a poem or two more enjoyable, but imagine having to read *War and Peace* that way.

Like your handwriting's idiosyncrasies, each font has its own way of doing things, with unique characteristics that set it apart from all the other fonts in the world. As a result, some are more appealing and more useful than others. In fact, a handful are just downright, um, eccentric. For example:

This one's called Linotext

Perfect for the Halloween edition of your company newsletter, but not exactly the Honda Civic of typestyles.

Which is what we want for our slides—the font equivalent of the Civic:

- practical
- popular
- efficient
- easy to handle

And just as with cars, knowing what we need in a font makes the process of choosing the right one a whole lot easier.

So, if the Civic were a font, what would it look like? That's easy:

- **clean lines**
- **simple not fancy**

Fortunately, there's a whole class of fonts that fit this description—they're called *sans serif*. "Sans" is Latin for "without" and "serif" rhymes with "sheriff."

Great. So what the bleep is a serif? And why don't we want them hanging around our fonts?

ser ● if   *n.*   The flourishes at the ends of a letter's main strokes

See for yourself. They're not all marked here, but you get the idea.

Here's the thing about serifs. They're great in small-scale media like newspapers, magazines, and novels, where the type is typically tiny. In such situations, serifs provide a level of detail that helps the human eye "lock on." Sort of like visual handlebars.

But as the media changes and the type gets larger, and certainly by the time you get to something on the scale of a street sign, highway sign, billboard—or **big screen presentation**—those previously-handy serifs are now just a whole lot of visual noise. What we need on screen is **simplicity**. Clean, even lines that just *end*. No drama. Like so:

Mmtg

This is why you never see street signs, highway signs, or even most billboards printed in anything other than a **sans serif** typeface.

Think about it. Which kind of highway sign do we usually see?

This?   **Or this?**

Los Angeles

.Next 137 exits

Los Angeles

Next 137 exits

Almost always the one on the right of course.

Why, then, does the text on our slides so often look like this . . .

Shopping List

✱ Sugar, spice

✱ Everything nice

✱ Snails, puppy dog tails

✱ Curds, whey

✱ Soy waffles w/ wheatgrass

✱ Extra whitening toothpaste

. . . instead of **this**?

Shopping List

* Sugar, spice
* Everything nice
* Snails, puppy dog tails
* Curds, whey
* Soy waffles w/ wheatgrass
* Extra whitening toothpaste

Sans serif fonts are considerably more readable on-screen than those in the **serif** category. See for yourself:

- pick one of your own slides and make copies to work with

- render one copy in a **sans serif** font and the other in **serif** (see the handy lists on the next page)

- run the slideshow on a full-size presentation screen

- switch back and forth between the two versions of the slide

- view them from various distances and in different lighting

- invite your colleagues in and get their opinions

- celebrate Nadine's birthday now that everybody's in one place

Some of the most common typefaces in both categories are displayed on the following page. Remember, the serif fonts will look good here because the printed page is their medium of choice. But put them on a big screen presentation and something gets lost in translation.

Times New Roman   Aa Bb Cc 1 2 3 $ % &

Bookman Oldstyle   Aa Bb Cc 1 2 3 $ % &

Garamond   Aa Bb Cc 1 2 3 $ % &

Georgia   Aa Bb Cc 1 2 3 $ % &

Palatino   Aa Bb Cc 1 2 3 $ % &

Century Schoolbook   Aa Bb Cc 1 2 3 $ % &

The most popular **sans serif** faces—and therefore our **best choices for onscreen legibility**—are the ones shown here.

Common Sans Serif Fonts

Arial   Aa Bb Cc 1 2 3 $ % &

Arial Narrow   Aa Bb Cc 1 2 3 $ % &

Avant Garde   Aa Bb Cc 1 2 3 $ % &

News Gothic   Aa Bb Cc 1 2 3 $ % &

Tahoma   Aa Bb Cc 1 2 3 $ % &

Trebuchet MS   Aa Bb Cc 1 2 3 $ % &

Verdana   Aa Bb Cc 1 2 3 $ % &

Those last two sans serif fonts are interesting critters. For its part, Trebuchet is by far the fanciest out of this standard stable of sans serif typefaces. While its characters don't feature serifs per se, I think it's fair to say that Trebuchet is a font with latent serif tendencies (not that there's anything wrong with that). It's a great choice when your slides need a little more jazz or sophistication than usual. Verdana, meanwhile, is extremely readable on screen, but its characters are friggin' huge. Letter for letter, Verdana takes up more horizontal real estate than almost any other font. But hey, choosing it is a great way to inoculate your slides against verbalitis. **Bonus tip:** Use 10-point Verdana regular (not bold) as your default font for email. It's hard to find anything clearer or more readable on the small screen.

If you must use a serif font for some compelling, unavoidable reason, then your best bet might be **Georgia**. It is among the most legible of serif fonts on screen, and for good reason—Microsoft commissioned its creation specifically for that purpose.

If used, serif typefaces are best displayed at large point sizes. Hence, one practical use for them is in **slide titles**, where they can provide an added touch of elegance if desired, as in this example:

On the following page is another Designer's Notebook entry, one that lets you record the names of the preferred sans serif typefaces you come across in your PowerPoint travels. There are a million typefaces out there, so it's a good idea to keep tabs on your faves.

Fonts

New fonts hit the electronic marketplace every week. Some are good, some are bad, and some are downright ugly. Problem is, there are so many out there that it's hard to keep track of them all. To make matters worse—and this is a proven scientific fact, mind you—no two computers in the world have exactly the same set of fonts installed on them. (I can't actually prove that, but I'm sure it's true).

As we discussed in this section, **sans serif** fonts are the best choice for onscreen readability. Use this page to keep a working list of the best screen fonts you come across. If you like, use the stars to mark your favorites.

Best Screen Fonts
(sans serif)

	Favorite		Favorite
_____	☆	_____	☆
_____	☆	_____	☆
_____	☆	_____	☆
_____	☆	_____	☆
_____	☆	_____	☆
_____	☆	_____	☆
_____	☆	_____	☆
_____	☆	_____	☆
_____	☆	_____	☆
_____	☆	_____	☆
_____	☆	_____	☆

Hide and Seek

If you need to **blank** the screen in order to better manage a conversation with the audience, there are two easy options, the B key or the W key.

The B key blacks out the screen. The W key whites it out.

Click any key or press the mouse button and the blank screen disappears.

To jump **DIRECTLY** to any slide **WITHOUT** having to **EXIT** the presentation, simply type the page number of that slide + the Enter key.

Craft a professional visual style

Do you recognize the clip-art on this page? Alas! You most certainly do. That's because each and every piece is a founding member of:

The Clip-Art

Need to show a red sports car? Try a photograph.

The rhetorical equivalent of giving your audience the finger

I'd hate to see what they give third place

He's climbed more mountains than all the Von Trapps combined

Not a single one of these colors occurs in nature

Welcome to Public Access Channel 17. Today's class: Advanced Graphic Design.

Of course these six pieces aren't the only Hall of Shamers, but it would take a dozen more pages just to scratch the surface of what's out there. How does one get to be in the Clip-Art Hall of Shame? Well, there happen to be some very strict criteria:

 They're almost as old as PowerPoint itself. Most of these have been in circulation since the early 1990s. That's 1,359 in computer years. Using them is like showing up at your 20th high school reunion in a Cadillac Cimarron.

 Like our mountain-climbing friend, they've been disgracing the faces of more slides than we can count. When an audience sees them today, it's like beginning your presentation by saying: *Hello. I'm incompetent. And I think I just soiled myself.*

 They look like they were drawn on a computer . . . *because they were.* Back in the day, even the most primitive graphics/**CAD** programs were cool. Today, those original programs and the people who still love them belong in museums.

 It's bad enough *looking* computer-generated, but Hall of Shamers are also cartoonish, cheesy, immature, unprofessional, amateurish, off-putting, puerile, and my editor says I have to stop now.

Today there are literally hundreds of thousands of excellent alternatives to this kind of schlock. Thankfully, one of the best sources is Microsoft itself vis-à-vis its **"Office Online"** site, which can be found at:

http://office.microsoft.com

There awaits a virtual smorgasbord of free, high-quality clip-art and photographs, all available for downloading and use (within proper limits, of course, but the terms are generous). Sometimes you have to look very hard to find just the right piece, but generally you can snag something that is both professional and appropriate to your needs.

It's important to correct the misperception that *all* clip-art is bad and should never be used. Instead, it's more accurate to say that:

a. *most* clip-art is bad

b. some clip-art is downright wonderful

c. if used, clip-art should fit audience, occasion, and mood

d. by *definition*, clip-art is a more *whimsical* choice than photography, so always weigh its appropriateness

Thankfully, a careful search of sites like Shutterstock suggests that the days of neon green money and sky blue sweaters are numbered:

**Shutterstock Image ID
83419651**

**Shutterstock Image ID
17636251**

**Shutterstock Image ID
91692797**

Choosing between clip-art and photographs depends on your analysis of the audience, your presentational goals, and other factors. But one thing is certain—because slides are a visual medium, **they require the presence of graphic elements** for maximum impact.

Clip-Art? Fine. Photographs? Great. Neither? **Not an option**.

Text simply must not be allowed to not dominate or overpower your slides. As pointed out repeatedly in the discussion of Rule 2, if you prefer to be text-intensive, use the printed page.

Speaking of photos and clip-art, what do all too many of the photographs used in slide presentations have in common with the piece of clip-art shown here?

Answer: They're **grainy** ─────────────────▶

(I'm not proud of that, but if it got your attention then it was worth it.)

Grainy and otherwise distorted images are the bane of slidewatching audiences everywhere. Take this, er, *lovely* stapler for instance:

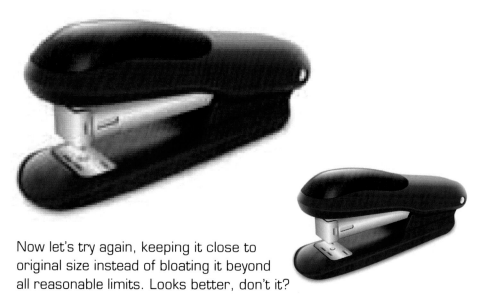

Now let's try again, keeping it close to original size instead of bloating it beyond all reasonable limits. Looks better, don't it?

If the original image is too small to work at large sizes, don't push it. Just keep looking until you find one that will.

Speaking of too small, can you tell what's going on in the photo on the right? Perhaps, but try doing so:

- from 50 feet away
- in harsh lighting
- when it's only on screen for 3 seconds
- and this is *actual size*

Grainy is one thing, but it's no better than the alternative—an image that's too small for audience members to cognitively process. Next time you're sizing a photo for use in a presentation, just ask yourself: **What would Goldilocks do?** Presumably, she'd always pick the image that was "just right."

But making photos too big or too small instead of just right isn't the only pet peeve audiences have with slide images. For example, notice anything odd about this photo of a famous American landmark?

Actually, there are two different problems—it is both stretched too far horizontally and compressed vertically. Here's the deal. Every straight-edged image has **eight** control points as seen in the correctly proportioned version of the photo shown at left on the next page:

However, to resize an image *and maintain its original proportionality, only the **corner** control points can be used* (see version at right). Dragging from any of the middle control points will produce an image that looks "squashed" or "stretched."

Not all photographs give the appearance of having straight edges, however. Neither, for that matter, does most clip-art. The rules for dealing with such "edge-less" images will be discussed in a moment.

In the meantime, flip back and see if you notice anything about the straight-edged images that have appeared so far in this book. They've all had two distinct formatting techniques applied to them.

Can you figure out what they are?

To check your guesses, consider this "raw" photograph that was imported from Shutterstock.

Save Our Slides

Every straight-edged image that gets put on a slide needs just a couple of finishing touches:

1. **A 1/4-point border**
2. **Drop shadow**

A 1/4-point line is the smallest border available in PowerPoint, and it does the job without calling undue attention to itself. I typically choose black unless the image itself requires the use of a different color. (Be sure to crop the image if there are any gaps between the edges of the image and the border lines.)

There are numerous variations on the basic idea of the shadow, but I almost always use the default lower-right drop shadow.

If we apply both of these simple techniques to our image of Mt. Fuji, we get first the left image and then the finished one on the right:

It is important to note, however, that not all images are meant to seem "framed" in this way. For example, look what happens when these three pieces are formatted with a border and shadow:

Such artificial borders serve no purpose. They just diminish the visual impact of the images they surround. With straight-edged photos like Mt. Fuji, a border "frames" the image and effectively gives it a formal, "finished" quality. Not so with open-ended images like this fire hydrant, bouquet, and kettle. Instead of framing and finishing, borders serve only to constrain them. If you have a slide with a white or very light background, leave "edge-less" images such as these unframed—they are most effective when allowed to naturally blend with the space around them.

That goes for a majority of traditional clip-art images as well (i.e., two-dimensional drawings). Don't run for a border. Just let them be:

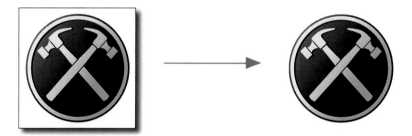

The ability to let such images blend in is a chief advantage of using templates with **white backgrounds** (as opposed to those with dark backgrounds). If this is not an option, however, the artificial fill color (white or otherwise) around the edges of many images can often be made to disappear using the "Set Transparent Color" option. (In Office for Windows, double click the graphic to call up the Picture Tools/ Format ribbon. Look for Recolor at the far left, then drop down to find the option for setting transparent color.) The image can then blend into a slide of any background color.

The third and final Designer's Notebook entry appears on the next page. This one is meant to help you keep track of your favorite clip-art style sets from Microsoft Office Online.

Clip-Art Styles

Microsoft's "Office Online" website contains thousands of drawings, graphics, illustrations, symbols, and other forms of clip-art. Many of these pieces share an intentionally similar visual style and were clearly drawn as a group so that they could complement each other within a single document or presentation. And that's a good thing. After all:

Using similar clip-art styles throughout a single slideshow is an excellent way to maximize the professionalism of your presentation.

Fortunately, Microsoft has given us an easy way to use this "single style" strategy. If a piece of clip-art found on Office Online is part of a family of similarly designed objects, it is assigned a **Style number**.

To determine if a piece of clip-art you like is part of a family, just click on its thumbnail image. A pop-up window will appear showing you a larger version of the graphic plus descriptive data, including the Style number if there is one. To see that entire style family, just click on the number (it's a link). There are a **lot** of styles, so use this page to keep track of the ones that interest you most.

Favorite		Favorite		Favorite	
_____	☆	_____	☆	_____	☆
_____	☆	_____	☆	_____	☆
_____	☆	_____	☆	_____	☆
_____	☆	_____	☆	_____	☆
_____	☆	_____	☆	_____	☆
_____	☆	_____	☆	_____	☆
_____	☆	_____	☆	_____	☆

Video Victory

Audiences are quite accepting of grainy, poor-quality video (thank you, World Wide Web). This paradox is great news for presenters because it means that, as long as the subject and content of the video is fitting, almost any clip can enhance the impact of a presentation.

There is only one caveat here: **It has to actually work.** If the video doesn't play, loses audio, hangs up, etc., then you risk looking unprepared, unprofessional, or, worst of all, incompetent. The best way to avoid such snafus is to use a **physical video file** rather than trying to link to or embed code from a video that resides online somewhere.

Assuming you aren't in violation of copyright and/or fair use laws, your chosen clip is best in one of the following PowerPoint-friendly video formats:

- **avi** (Windows Video File)
- **wmv** (Windows Media Video)
- **mov** (Quicktime—Mac users only)

ONE MORE THING: Any video clip "inserted" on a slide must be present in a separate file alongside your PowerPoint presentation. Despite appearances, the videos aren't actually contained IN your slides. What looks like a video on a slide is just a placeholder that points to where the actual video resides.

There are other potentially compatible file types, but choosing them is, in my opinion, asking for trouble. If you need to convert an existing video into .avi or .wmv format, consider using a program like **Microsoft Expression Encoder**. Mac users, to create .wmv files you need to install the **Flip4Mac** QuickTime video codecs. Installing the codecs for **viewing** .wmv files is free, but to convert such files into .mov format (or vice versa) may require a software purchase.

Rule 5: **COLOR**

Always use high-contrast combinations

How many presentations have you sat through where it was ALMOST IMPOSSIBLE TO SEE the text . . .

. . . even with the lights off . . .

. . . from the front row?

The fifth Rule of Design exists because the answer to this question is inevitably, "too many."

I'm convinced that speakers don't intentionally mean to torment their audiences by using weak color combinations. It happens so frequently that there has to be some other explanation.

And there is.

Here's what's going on. When making slides, presenters are almost always looking at a **small screen**, be it a laptop display or a desktop monitor.

But these are **high-resolution** devices, so much so that even the poorest color combinations can be clearly seen.

So as presenters make slides, it doesn't occur to them that some color choices **might not translate well** to big screen projection systems.

The typical projection screen has a much lower resolution than a small monitor. Brightness is greatly diminished, as are the depth and richness of colors.

In other words, our slides often appear "washed out" on screen when compared to the vibrant colors that our small monitors produce.

Thankfully, the solution to this problem is a simple one. When making slides, presenters should check the color of the **text** against the color of its **background** to ensure that one of two conditions is always true:

Dark text is on a light background

and/or . . .

Light text is on a dark background

As long as one of these conditions is true for every item of text on your slides, then by definition you're using a **high-contrast** color combination. As a result, no matter what the physical condition of the venue you're presenting in—overhead lighting, projector quality, etc.—more likely than not, the audience will be able to read the text on your slides (unless it's in 14-point Times New Roman, in which case, you're already your own worst enemy).

Just think of it. No more vain attempts to decipher:

yellow text on a white background

gray text on a black background

white text on a cyan background

red text on a brown background

Text colors and background colors should be VERY whatever they are—namely **very** dark or **very** light, and each the opposite of the other (one dark, the other light).

But beware the temptation to interpret merely BRIGHT colors as being LIGHT colors. Visually, they're different parameters—one has to do with hue, the other with saturation.

You might remember a line from *Ghostbusters* that went something like, "Whatever you do, don't cross the streams. That would be bad." The Rules of Design feature a similar saying:

Don't mix the brights

In other words, keep **bright text** colors and **bright background** colors AWAY from each other. Don't mix them. Don't cross them. If you do, it will be bad. See for yourself.

Ladies and gentlemen, I give you the phenomenon known as:

Simultaneous contrast

And in case you were wondering, it "works" the other way too:

Simultaneous contrast

Don't merely glance. **Stare** at both of these boxes for a while. The reason the text in these swatches appears to be "buzzing" is this—our brains don't know whether the red or the blue belongs in the foreground. As a result, we're assigning **both** colors to the foreground at the same time. By the way, it's bad enough here in a staring contest with a printed page, but try these combos for real the next time you're making slides. The effects are much more pronounced on actual screens.

And, as you will see, it's a bad thing.

Then again, it would certainly make an interesting attention getter for your next presentation.

Putting It All Together

Consider the following slide:

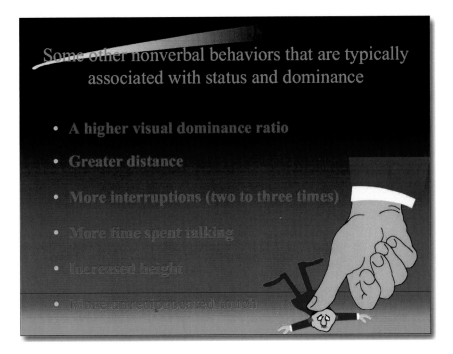

Scary, ain't it? Well its atrocious stylings are the pride and joy of my good friend and graduate school mentor, who deliberately breaks all of the Rules of Design just to irritate me. By the way, it was his idea to base this exercise on one of his slides.

Here's the assignment. Study this slide in light of the first five Rules of Design presented in this book, then on the following page list all of the things that are wrong with it (in any order). Note that there probably aren't 15 separate things wrong with this slide, but you never know. Besides, we had the room to put 15 lines on the next page, so we did. Happy hunting.

1. _____

2. _____

3. _____

4. _____

5. _____

6. _____

7. _____

8. _____

9. _____

10. _____

11. _____

12. _____

13. _____

14. _____

15. _____

Auto <u>In</u>-correct

By default, PowerPoint tries to be helpful in a variety of ways by guessing what it's just sure you were going to do anyway and then pre-emptively doing it for you. As my friend Mo Brantley would wisely (and sarcastically) ask:

"What could possibly go wrong?"

Oooooh, a couple of things, as it turns out. Namely, automatically resizing text and titles in order to "make room" for new content you're trying to add to an existing slide. I don't know about you, but I hate it when any of that stuff happens.

And it used to happen a lot, until I discovered I could tell PowerPoint to stop deciding such things for me. Here's how.

1. Find the program's "**Options**" function (under "File" in Windows)

2. Then choose "**Proofing**" and click "**AutoCorrect Options** . . ." as shown

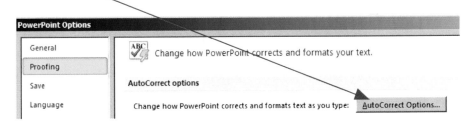

3. Flip this page over to the back side, as we ain't quite done yet

---

4. Almost there! Click the tab "**AutoFormat As You Type**"—

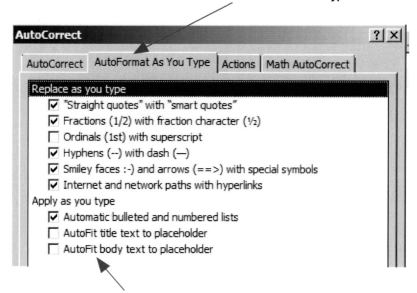

5. It's only the **last two items** on this list that we're concerned about

6. **Uncheck them!**

7. They're checked by default, so unless someone else uses your computer, it's unlikely you'll find them turned off. If they *are* already off when you get there, it might be time to find out who else has been touching your stuff.

While you're at it, click the "AutoCorrect" tab just to make sure that there isn't some other thing that PowerPoint is doing for you that you'd rather do yourself.

And don't worry. This can't be counted against you when people try to bring up your control issues.

Rule 6: **ANIMATION**

Resist the urge to get all crazy

When we were growing up and our moms encouraged us to be creative, going bonkers with PowerPoint's endless animation possibilities was not what they had in mind. And while I've never actually met your mom, I don't have to. Trust me on this. She agrees with everything I'm about to say.

Consider the following philosophical questions. Had he thought of it first, I'm sure Plato would have christened this the "Art thou really, truly certain of that?" method.

- Do we really need to see what a line of text looks like

  . . . ***backwards***

  . . . while ***spinning***?

REALLY?

- Do we really need to see text come ***bouncing*** in one word (or, Heaven help us, one letter) at a time, like Jack Russell puppies hopped up on catnip?

REALLY?

- Do we really need to . . . Oh my gosh! That text is . . . is ***zooming***. *It's coming right for us!*

REALLY?

- Do we really need to see things ***fly in*** from here, there, and everywhere, for the 8,700th time?

Mayday!

REALLY?

Speaking of Plato, he is believed by some people (i.e., me) to be the source of the following gem of slide design wisdom. If true, the Plat-man was way ahead of his time.

Animation effects
should REVEAL things
not REVEL in them.

Good design only REVEALS content; it never REVELS in it. Reveling is for life, for love, for parties, and for puppies. Not for bullets on a presentation screen. Recall the principle of transparency, namely that good design does not draw undue attention to itself. That means no flying, crazy zooming, bouncing, fencing, or basket weaving.

In fact, for the record, audiences the world over would like to **prohibit** bullets, text boxes, and most other slide-based objects from engaging in **any** of the following activities. To do so should be considered a perversion of the electronic order.

FLY FLUTTER LEAP

CRUISE SAIL DIVE

GALLOP RACE SPIN

As the preceding list suggests, the general rule for evaluating animation effects is this:

If it moves, **SHOOT** it.

Unless you **need** to move an object, choose animation effects that don't require your content to change ZIP codes in order to get to where it's going. A little animation is one thing, but MOVEMENT is something else entirely. Animation effects that fea-  ture a significant amount of screen movement have a special name: **distracting**.

Recently the FBI may (or may not) have published their "**10 Most Unwanted**" list for animation effects. Not surprisingly, "Fly In" was Public Animation Enemy Number 1. And it's in good company. Here's the complete list:

1. Fly In	9. Magnify
2. Crawl In	10. Fold
3. Swivel	11. Float
4. Bounce	12. Light Speed
5. Spiral In	13. Credits
6. Center Revolve	14. Flip
7. Rise Up	15. Swish
8. Boomerang	16. Pinwheel

Apparently, the FBI needs more accountants. By the way, even though **Fly In** is the worst offender on the list by virtue of its being abused far more than any other, make no mistake: Using any of these movement-heavy effects to animate text is a bad idea.

Why? As mentioned above, they violate the prime directive of good design—transparency—by calling the audience's attention to the effect rather than the content. **Good design never competes with its own content for the audience's attention.** In addition, there are three more good reasons not to use these kinds of effects for handling text:

1. **AMATEURISH**: Such choices suggest that the speaker isn't terribly experienced—an attribution that no presenter can afford. It's an instant credibility-shrinker for the speaker, and, for the audience, an instant enthusiasm-shrinker.

2. **UNPROFESSIONAL**: Even worse than looking like an amateur, seeming unprofessional communicates something else to the audience—something quite unintended but also quite damning: **disrespect**.

3. **TIME CONSUMING**: Audiences don't want (or deserve) to wait while our bullets c-r-a-w-l across the screen. Also, as speakers, what are we supposed to do during this time "in transit"—tell jokes? (So did you hear the one about the two text boxes who walked into a bar chart?)

At this point, of course, we're in danger of begging the obvious question—what are the characteristics of GOOD animation effects? There are three things to look for:

1. **LOW-KEY**: The effect does not call attention to itself.

2. **STATIONARY**: Minimal left/right or up/down movement.

3. **QUICK**: Wastes no time—the audience's or yours.

You might be wondering what build effects I use. Thought you'd never ask! Unless I have a good reason not to, I default to "**Fade**" set at "**Very fast**" speed. If I'm feeling the love and/or have had too much cough syrup before bedtime, I will occasionally allow myself to use the following:

- Expand
- Compress

- Ascend
- Descend
- Wipe
- Strips
- Split

> # ACHTUNG, BABY!
> **All guidelines mentioned in this chapter apply equally to entrance & exit effects alike.**

There are other acceptable choices that still manage to meet the three criteria above, but it's hard to go wrong with any of the members of "Fade and the Super Seven" (a name I made up just now). And as the box above suggests, IF you need to use **exit** effects (I'm not saying that you do), Fade and the Super Seven still represent your best stable of choices.

Having come so far, however, there is still one final warning to heed lest all your hard work and excellent choices amount to naught.

Sound effects—you know, the ones that come with PowerPoint?

They suck.

Do not use them.

No *explosions*.

No *drum rolls*.

No *cha-chings*.

No *friggin' gunfire*.

No *tires peeling*.

No *camera clicks*.

No *chimes*.

No *clapping*.

No *breaking glass*.

No *applause*
(other than what you earn from the audience the old-fashioned way).

- ## Do I need to use animation effects at all?

  Definitely. Using entrance effects puts you in control of the narrative, and, as speaker, that's your job. Don't let the audience pick and choose where to direct their attention. This isn't Craigslist or window shopping. It's a live guided tour and you're the tour guide. By not using entrance effects to introduce talking points, you risk the audience reading ahead and getting distracted by something you haven't even had the chance to put into context yet.

- ## So I should use entrance effects. What about exit effects?

  Exit effects aren't generally necessary. Once you've introduced your talking points, leaving them in place is useful because it helps audiences remember the overall narrative and how its various parts fit together. However, this notion only applies to text. If you have a lot of IMAGES to cycle through on a given slide, then using exit effects to avoid clutter is a necessity.

- ## What about dimming bullets as you move down a list?

  Better than exiting them off-screen altogether, but still not recommended. Audiences are pretty darn good at keeping up with you. And even though it seems counterintuitive, there's something about dimming bullets that makes some audience members want to "go back" and see what they missed— almost as if you're daring them to do so. If that happens then you've lost control of the presentation.

- ## Is using a variety of animation effects in a presentation okay?

  You can, if you wish, use different effects for different categories of objects—for example: Fade for text bullets, Descend for standalone text boxes, and Faded Zoom for images. But within a category, strive for consistency. A consistent visual style can't be overrated as it's an attribute that speaks directly to your professionalism, and hence, your credibility as a presenter.

- ## Aren't the animation rules different for images?

  A little bit. First, it's worth noting that Fade and the Super Seven effects work just as well for images as they do for bullets and text boxes, so don't stray from them unless you just can't help it. And if you just can't help it, don't venture much beyond Zoom, Faded Zoom, or Grow and Turn. Also, as I mention above, it's often a good idea to use exit effects when working with multiple images on a slide in order to prevent clutter, and to manage the narrative more efficiently. However, having said all that, one rule remains inviolate: no Fly In (or Fly Out) effect.

- ## What about using random effects?

  Only if you like playing Russian Roulette with your audience's nerves.

- ## Why would Microsoft put most of the offending effects under a category called "Exciting"?

  It's either the height of irony or a typo. Here's my theory: One day at Microsoft, a programmer became distracted by a text message or a low-flying plane, glanced away from the computer, and inadvertently omitted four letters while trying to type the word "Excruciating."

Beautiful Bookends

Every slideshow needs nice front and back covers, or what I call "bookend" slides.

If nothing else, you can use the traditional title slide layout that comes with your template to type a title and subtitle.

Click to add title

Click to add subtitle

Eh. Color me unimpressed.

While technically better than nothing, this approach is so commonplace and pedestrian it could bore a dog. And if a dog can be bored by it, imagine how your audience probably feels.

Instead, let go of the template (just ignore it) for your opening and closing cover slides and use **stunning full-screen images** instead.

Think of them as the **glossy front and back covers** of a brochure or a beautiful set of bookends bracketing items on a shelf (sorry about all of the Bs in this sentence). When done well, they give a presentation a "finished" look, saying to your audience, in effect, "I put some real effort into this presentation." The attitudinal differences in the way your audience perceives you and your message are probably impossible to measure, but they're there and they're real. Believe me. And since seeing is believing, see below for some examples.

In this case, let's assume you're part of a company or organization named "LOREM," and that spiffy blue-green thing is your logo or symbol.

A black or dark bookend can be striking and memorable. Remember, this is a cover slide, not a template, so using a dark background color is just fine.

At the end of the presentation, just use the same cover slide again (hence the term "bookends"). Bring up the closing bookend slide when you say your goodbyes and thank-yous or move into a question-and-answer session. **Never just END a presentation on your last content slide.** To paraphrase Martha Stewart, "That would be a bad thing."

Of course, you could get a little more creative if the occasion merits. If the subject of your presentation has something to do with transportation, for example, consider using a pair of complementary bookends that visually imply beginning and ending:

 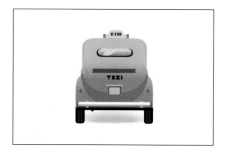

Infusing your bookends with this kind of visual logic is an opportunity to creatively grab and hold an audience's attention. That said, such an approach is inherently more whimsical than simply showing the logo at the beginning and end. So, make sure that whatever you do fits the occasion. Here's hoping you'll have an opportunity to use visual pairings like these:

Rule 7: cApiTaLIzaTiOn

Not everything needs to be capitalized

Last chapter, we traded on Plato's ethos. This time it's that of Shakespeare, who has many famous phrases attributed to him. One saying that has not been attributed to him (yet) is the following:

To capitalize or not to capitalize.

That is the question.

Ain't that the truth. In PowerPoint, it's the question we face every time we type a title, a line of text, or a single piece of text in a box.

The answer, which may come as a surprise to many, is **NO** most of the time.

Just as in other media—writing, for instance—capital letters are a special case (pardon the pun) that are only used to confer status on a few words in a given passage. Consider this excerpt from Lewis Carroll's timeless classic, rendered the way we normally would in English, using what's called "Sentence" case capitalization rules:

"In THAT direction," the Cat said, waving its right paw round, "lives a Hatter: and in THAT direction," waving the other paw, "lives a March Hare. Visit either you like: they're both mad."

There are 33 words in this passage. Of these, exactly eight are capitalized, including two made entirely of capitals. This means that only about 25% of the words have special status, conferred on the basis of position (first word), need for emphasis, or rank (proper nouns). Without such status, **meaning is obscured**, and readers have

to **work harder** to interpret the author's original intent. For example:

"in that direction," the cat said, waving its right paw round, "lives a hatter: and in that direction," waving the other paw, "lives a march hare. visit either you like: they're both mad."

Just doesn't have the same punch, does it? Not a problem if you're texting someone, but definitely less than desirable in more formal settings. But just as there's more than one way to skin a Cheshire Cat, there's more than one way to misuse capitalization in ways that obscure meaning. Have another look. This is called "Start" case, but if you're using it, please "Stop"—

"In THAT Direction," The Cat Said, Waving Its Right Paw Round, "Lives A Hatter: And In THAT Direction," Waving The Other Paw, "Lives A March Hare. Visit Either You Like: They're Both Mad."

In Start case, every word is capitalized. As a result, the entire thing looks like one big title, not a paragraph of prose. None of us would ever write a paragraph this way—and yet **people do it all the time on slides**. Not only is Start case actually harder to read than all lowercase, it also makes capitals meaningless. This observation occasions a colored box:

If Everything Is Capitalized, Capital Letters Mean Nothing

If this is our approach to capitalization, there's no point bothering with it at all. The idea of special status goes out the window. We need some words to be more important than others, at least visually, in order to communicate more effectively.

And don't confuse Start case with "Title" case. We love Title case, which caps the first word and everything else EXCEPT prepositions, conjunctions, and articles. For example, in 1984 Douglas Adams published the fourth book in his *Hitchhiker* series, and because he used Title case it looks correct to our eye:

So Long, and Thanks for All the Fish

Not capitalized: prepositions, conjunctions, and articles

Oh, but we're not done yet. There's one more iteration of ineptitude to explore, namely the practice of ALL-CAPPING:

"IN THAT DIRECTION," THE CAT SAID, WAVING ITS RIGHT PAW ROUND, "LIVES A HATTER: AND IN THAT DIRECTION," WAVING THE OTHER PAW, "LIVES A MARCH HARE. VISIT EITHER YOU LIKE: THEY'RE BOTH MAD."

Once again, the value of capitalization as a communication strategy is negated. All-capping is also extremely hard on the eyes—and the brain. That's because we read English words largely on the basis of appearance—the distinctive shapes produced when lowercase letters combine with the occasional uppercase. Lowercase letters are easier to distinguish from one another than uppercase letters are from other uppercase letters, as can be seen easily enough in this comparison:

a b c d e f g h i j k l m n o p q r s t u v w x y z

A B C D E F G H I J K L M N O P Q R S T U V W X Y Z

Some uppercase letters share similar shapes, making them harder to differentiate as individual characters, and hence harder to read. For instance, consider the following list of three items that many troubled organizations might aspire to, and hence turn into a presentation slide at a meeting. Here it is in Arial typeface:

• Recoup core crop	• RECOUP CORE CROP
• Regroup web code	• REGROUP WEB CODE
• Regrow proud force	• REGROW PROUD FORCE

The relative desirability of the Sentence case version on the left is evident even on this high-resolution printed page. But if you're at a computer, try the same experiment. You'll find the difference even more noticeable. Using all-caps occasionally for EMPHASIS is fine ("Regrow PROUD force"), but as with all forms of emphasis (underlining, bolding, etc.) one should use all-caps SPARINGLY.

So what's a slide maker to do? Now that you know some of the lingo and the theory behind it, applying the following rules is a straightforward proposition:

1. For Slide Titles Use Title Case

2. For main bullets use Sentence case

3. In sub-bullets capitalize proper nouns only

4. For SPECIAL emphasis only, use all-caps as needed

To illustrate these rules, consider the two slides below. Which one is correct? And which one looks better? (Trick question: the correct slide should also look better).

Here they are again, larger and with commentary to point out the differences:

☑ Correct

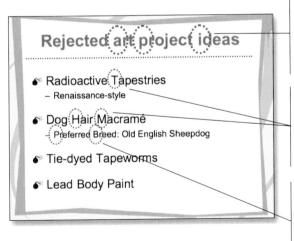

Rejected Art Project Ideas

🎇 Radioactive tapestries
  – Renaissance-style

🎇 Dog hair macramé
  – preferred breed: Old English Sheepdog

🎇 Tie-dyed tapeworms

🎇 Lead body paint

Title Case:
Every word capitalized except for prepositions, conjunctions, articles, and small land animals.

Sentence Case:
Capitalize only first word and proper nouns. Use ALL-CAPS for special emphasis only.

Sub-bullets:
ONLY proper nouns are capitalized. Rule also applies to first word. ALL-CAPS okay for special emphasis only.

⊘ Incorrect

Rejected art project ideas

🎇 Radioactive Tapestries
  – Renaissance-style

🎇 Dog Hair Macramé
  – Preferred Breed: Old English Sheepdog

🎇 Tie-dyed Tapeworms

🎇 Lead Body Paint

Mistake:
Using Sentence case in the title is too informal. Titles should look like titles not sentences.

Boo-boo:
As the keyworded remnants of full sentences, only first word and proper nouns should be capitalized.

Ouchie:
At sub-bullet level, ONLY proper nouns are capitalized. By definition sub-bullets are less important than main bullets and this should be reflected visually.

- ## What about punctuation on slides?

  Take another look at the previous slides and note one more correct design attribute they both share in common— a decided lack of punctuation. **Bullets and sub-bullets are keywords—not actual sentences. As a result, we don't owe them any punctuation.** Visually, adding periods to bullets and sub-bullets simply adds to a slide's clutter—something we're trying to produce less of not more.

  Note well that ending periods are OUT. Keywords eliminate the need for them.

  The occasional question mark is okay if in fact you're asking a question. Question marks are best used, however, if the main bullets (or the sub-bullets) on a given slide are **all** phrased as questions.

  The occasional internal comma is fine if you're listing things, but no terminal commas at the end of lines.

  Also, exclamation marks are a bad idea! Really! Avoid them! They make you look desperate! Amateurish! Unprofessional!

- ## Is it okay to combine all-caps and bolding to give extra special emphasis to a particular word?

  Sure, but don't get carried away. As special words go, anything you double-up on like that better be pretty friggin' spectacularly important.

- **Is it strictly necessary to capitalize the first word of main bullets?**

  Not strictly, no, because main bullets are not actual sentences, only the keyworded vestiges of them. If your own personal style demands it, feel free to leave those first words lowercase—unless, of course, they're proper nouns. Three caveats, however:

  One, realize that the vast majority of presenters do it the way I described in this chapter, so doing otherwise may look a little odd to your audience, and that means you're taking the risk of distracting them.

  Two, whatever visual style you adopt when it comes to capitalization, be consistent from slide to slide to slide.

  Three, not capitalizing the first word of a bullet conveys a more informal sense than using traditional Sentence case does. Hence, if formality is inherent in the context of your presentation, then you're well advised to stick with the approach described in this chapter.

It's Transition Time

There are actually two kinds of transitions that presenters often overlook. One type is visual and super easy to do. The other kind is verbal and unique to the content of a given presentation. Super important, but not particularly easy.

Let's take it easy to start. By visual transitions what I officially mean is **visual transitions between slides**. And there's only one as far as I'm concerned. Under "**Transitions**" choose "**Fade**" then go to "**Effect Options ▼**," and select "**Through Black**" as shown here:

And, yes, there are other transition effects, but they tend to draw too much attention to themselves—which is why I only have eyes for Fade Through Black.

See? I told you it was easy. *But there is one last thing.* BEFORE selecting this effect, **highlight all of your slides**. This step is illustrated on the next page using a sample presentation about ancient buildings. And while you're at it, be sure to check out those awesome, avant-garde bookend slides.

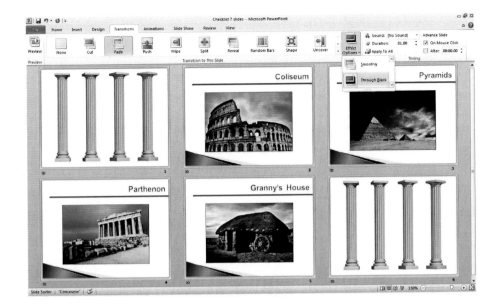

Visual transitions impart a sense of connectedness to the slides in a presentation, allowing each one to flow smoothly into the next. As it turns out, verbal transitions do the same thing for the ideas contained in those slides. Only they're a lot harder to implement.

First, understand that words and phrases like next, moving on, in addition, now then, and also DO NOT constitute the kind of verbal transitions I'm talking about. Those would be easy. They're also meaningless.

The main ideas in your body need to be connected by meaningful verbal transitions—logical bridges that explain how we got from the previous slide to the current slide. I'm NOT talking about getting from your introduction to your first main idea or from your last main idea to the closing. Those are technical verbal transitions that tend to take care of themselves (e.g., "to begin" and "in closing").

Rather, how does Main Idea 1 connect logically to Main Idea 2 and how does Main Idea 2 connect logically to Main Idea 3? And so on. Unfortunately, you'd be surprised at how often these important elements are simply omitted.

But it's a big problem for presenters. After all, if speakers can't clearly articulate the connection between main ideas/slides, why should they expect it to be obvious to their audience?

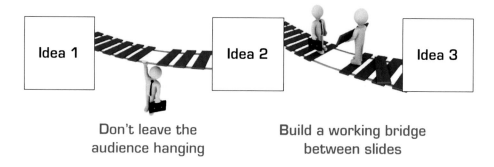

| Don't leave the audience hanging | Build a working bridge between slides |

It's practically a given that there exists some kind of meaningful relationship between any two ideas in the same speech. And that's the key. Find the relationship and use it as the basis for the verbal transition. Relationships are many and varied. Don't limit yourself to **cause-and-effect** (unless of course it's the right answer). Consider these formal relationships as well:

- **Time** (including before/after)
- **Antithesis** (opposition, including compare/contrast)
- **General-to-specific** (or vice versa)
- **Problem-solution**
- **Increasing superiority** (or vice versa)
- **Spatial** (including geography)

Suppose you're talking about a company with three seemingly unrelated divisions: office supplies, sporting goods, and organic foods. Depending on the specific details of the scenario, you could, for example, contrast the performance of the office supplies division with the sporting goods division, or you could arrange all three in order from poorest performance to the best performance. If a relationship doesn't present itself eventually, then try rearranging the order of the slides/ideas. In the end, you don't have to link all of your main ideas directly to each other, you simply have to find the bridge that gets you from one slide to the next in a logical and meaningful way.

About the Author

Not especially useful but still worth reading

Dr. William "Billy" Earnest is an Assistant Professor of Communication at St. Edward's University in Austin, Texas. He has Ph.D. and Master's degrees from The University of Texas at Austin, where he taught as an Assistant Instructor from 1997 until 2001. His doctoral work focused on the vagaries of electronic slides as a communication medium.

From 2002 to 2005 he was on the faculty of UT's prestigious McCombs School of Business, where he lectured in Business Communication and was nominated for a Texas Exes Outstanding Teaching Award.

Courses he has taught to date include:

- Media and Professional Presentations
- Business Communication
- Persuasion
- Presentational Speaking
- Communication and Culture
- Rhetorical Criticism

In 2005, he and two of his former business students founded SlideWise Design & Consulting, LLC, dedicated to the mission of reforming the way slides are made.

Dr. Earnest hails from Wichita Falls, Texas, home of his Alma Mater, Midwestern State University. From 1990 to 1995, he was an Atlanta-based systems analyst, technical writer, and corporate trainer for Electronic Data Systems.